Beyond Burnout

Regain Your Passion and Energy

GREGORY L. JANTZ, PHD
WITH KEITH WALL

Beyond Burnout:
Regain Your Passion and Energy

Published by Aspire Press
An imprint of Tyndale House Ministries
Carol Stream, Illinois
www.hendricksonrose.com

ISBN: 978-1-4964-8127-6

The views and opinions expressed in this book are those of the author(s) and do not necessarily express the views of Tyndale House Ministries or Aspire Press, nor is this book intended to be a substitute for mental health treatment or professional counseling. The information in this resource is intended as a guideline for healthy living. Please consult qualified medical, legal, pastoral, and psychological professionals regarding individual concerns.

Tyndale House Ministries and Aspire Press are in no way liable for any content, change of content, or activity for the works listed. Citation of a work does not mean endorsement of all its contents or of other works by the same author.

Printed in China by APS
April 2024, 1st Printing

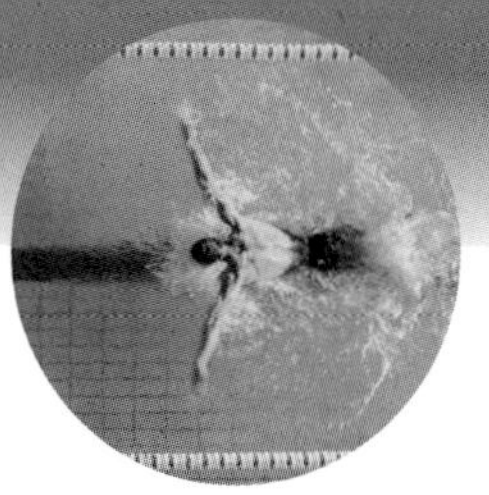

Contents

Introduction Running on Empty....5

Key 1 Streamline Your Stress.... 19

Key 2 Reclaim Your True Self.... 31

Key 3 Find Sanity through Simplicity 41

Key 4 Bolster Your Body 53

Key 5 Fortify Your Filters.... 71

Key 6 Choose to Replenish Yourself.... 83

A Closing Word The Master of Balance.... 101

Notes 107

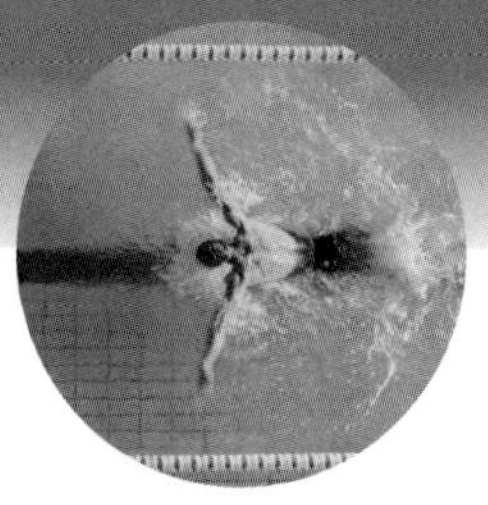

INTRODUCTION

Running on Empty

For the vast majority of people, life is hectic, stressful, and exhausting.

With the pressures of working a regular job, caring for kids or parents (maybe even at the same time), keeping up with household chores, and juggling community commitments, it's no surprise that so many people feel depleted.

Still, to some, the real meaning of *burnout* is quickly becoming vague and abstract. Many people use the term to communicate they've lost patience with an activity or have grown bored with a monotonous task. We hear these kinds of sentiments expressed on a regular basis:

- "I watched my sister's kids all weekend—talk about burnout!"

- "I've been remodeling the bathroom every weekend for a month. I'm burned-out on this project."
- "I'm getting burned-out by all this political nonsense."

But as a mental health professional for the past forty years, I resist using this word as an impersonal diagnosis, assigned with professional detachment or superiority.

Burnout in the mental health sense is a serious and significant condition that can leave a person chronically drained of energy, lacking motivation to do nearly anything, unable to sleep soundly, apathetic toward relationships, and sliding into poor health habits.

NONE OF US ARE STUCK IN A PLACE OF EXHAUSTION AND DESPAIR WITHOUT HOPE THAT THINGS WILL GET BETTER.

What's more, burnout often contributes to other problematic conditions, such as depression, anxiety, and addiction. Millions of Americans suffer from its all-too-real effects.

Over the years, I've learned an enormous amount about the psychological and physiological science of this condition by treating clients at the clinic I direct and by reading scores of research studies.

But by far, the lessons I value most are those I learned the hard way, from the inside out. I understand firsthand how deep the black hole of burnout can go and how dark it can get—because I've been there:

- I know how it feels to wake up in the morning and wonder where the energy will come from to get through the day.
- I have looked out at the once-vibrant world and seen only shades of gray, dull and flattened.
- I have felt the desperate and terrifying impulse to run away from life, as fast and as far as my legs would carry me.

If you recognize these feelings in yourself, you know very well that the answers you seek aren't easy or simple—or you would have found them already.

But what you may not know is that burnout is *not* the end of the story; it is *not* a life sentence. None of us are stuck in a place of exhaustion and despair without hope that things will get better. You *can* heal and regain the joy and vitality you once had. How can I be so sure? Because if I can do it, anyone can.

Wounded Healer

In the early 1980s, I had already launched The Center: A Place of Hope, a Seattle-area clinic specializing in the treatment of depression, anxiety, eating disorders, and other mental health issues. The effectiveness of our work with struggling individuals had drawn broad attention, and my team and I had begun to develop the "whole person" model for helping people heal when other methods had fallen short. As we refined this approach, our clients achieved substantial progress with our guidance and their own hard work.

Soon, more and more desperate individuals sought help at the clinic, and my calendar became overcrowded with frequent consultations, media opportunities, and speaking engagements. I was busy advising others how to take charge of their health and lifestyle habits—while my own were rapidly falling apart.

Working six days a week at a grueling (and foolish) pace, I had begun to make the classic mistake of not practicing what I preached. My diet was a wreck, and I made no attempt to exercise. I started to self-medicate with false comforts like junk food, excessive caffeine, and other unhealthy choices.

Nighttime became a nightmare of insomnia and crippling anxiety. Days were not much better—a deep emotional apathy and physical lethargy overtook my waking hours. Not surprisingly, my spiritual life was coming unglued as well. For decades my Christian faith had been a source of joy and guidance, but now it felt like an obligation—another set of to-dos occupying my endless checklist.

In spite of continued success in my psychology practice, I began to fear I'd chosen the wrong vocation. I even planned my escape to Colorado Springs, a city far away from our home in coastal Washington. My family had vacationed there when I was a child, so it seemed like a safe oasis amid the chaos.

After months of this descent into burnout, something happened that changed things for the better. My lifeline came, ironically enough, in the form of total exhaustion. The people who cared about me most stepped in to steer me back on course, demonstrating equal measures of loving support and tough love.

Family members and close friends helped me develop a rigid daily regimen that included shortened workdays, regular walks, improved sleep habits, a nutritious diet, time for prayer and reflection, playtime with my wife and boys, and much more.

I had to set new boundaries, and I committed to sticking with my support team. And so began my long climb back to health and well-being. Along the way, I gained the confidence to say, without a shred of doubt, that you can heal too.

A Closer Look at Burnout

Burnout was first used to describe a condition that develops after a cycle of severe stress, often affecting people who help others in a professional setting, such as social workers, nurses, and firefighters.

The term was popularized in the mid-1970s by psychologist Herbert Freudenberger after he observed how volunteers working at free medical clinics were losing motivation and becoming emotionally depleted. Dr. Freudenberger himself experienced a similar crisis in his own work at a New York City clinic he had started.[1]

In subsequent years, research has confirmed that burnout affects not only service providers working in intense environments, but also teachers, parents, college students, baristas, construction workers, landscapers, and beekeepers. In short, all of society. The fact is, we live in a culture that is ...

- Fast-paced and getting faster all the time
- Overwhelmed with options and decisions
- Inundated with information and digital stimuli

- Constantly stressed without recognizing the need for rest and renewal
- Obsessed with achievement and accomplishments, often at the cost of personal wellness

BURNOUT IS CAUSED BY PROLONGED STRESS ACROSS A SPECTRUM OF LIFE SITUATIONS.

Psychology Today's definition of *burnout* demonstrates its broad impact: "Burnout is a state of emotional, mental, and often physical exhaustion brought on by prolonged or repeated stress. Though it's most often caused by problems at work, it can also appear in other areas of life, such as parenting, caretaking, or romantic relationships."[2]

This definition highlights an important point: Most people think of burnout as it relates to the workplace, and it's true that job stress is one of the most common sources of emotional, mental, and physical exhaustion. But to be more accurate, burnout is caused by prolonged stress across a *spectrum* of life situations.

If you are currently on the verge of burnout, you are not alone. And if you are experiencing full-blown burnout, you are also not alone. Burnout is not the experience of a few; it has become the experience of the majority. Consider the following statistics:

- One survey found that 70 percent of workers had experienced burnout over the previous year, with 84 percent of Gen Zers and 74 percent of Millennials reporting burnout.[3]
- In another survey, 68 percent of non-executives and 81 percent of executives said that improving their well-being was more important than advancing their careers.[4]
- Recently, 38 percent of pastors polled by the Barna Group reported they had considered quitting full-time ministry due to fatigue and burnout—a 9 percent increase from the previous year.[5]

Rising Levels of Stress

According to the American Psychological Association, the combined result of recent pandemics, global conflict, natural disasters, and economic uncertainty can be likened to "impacts of a collective trauma." Health concerns, finances, and family responsibilities rank as the top daily stressors. Stress levels also seem higher among younger people, with Gen Zers and Millennials reporting the highest average levels of stress.[6]

Complicating the situation is that ironically enough, innovations originally designed to make life easier—advances in technology, for example—often add to our sense of being overwhelmed. As technology expert Bernard Marr explains,

> Our brains are being expected to cope with data flowing into them from all directions as our computers, smart phones and connected devices constantly beep, flash and bombard us with information.... Our brains aren't built to cope with the ever-increasing volumes of data we are trying to cram into them—and this is leading to brain malfunction in the form of stress.[7]

What is the impact of all this stress? One nationwide survey showed that approximately a third of adult respondents "reported that stress is completely overwhelming most days." The top negatively affected areas include mental health, eating habits, physical health, and interest in hobbies and activities.[8]

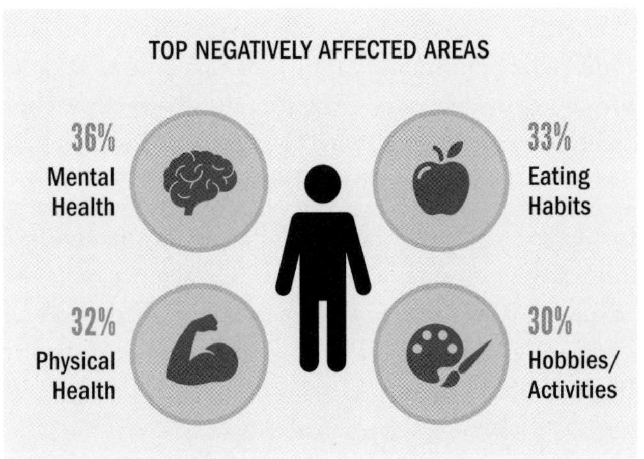

What the Science Says

Numerous research studies, spanning from the present day to many decades in the past, demonstrate conclusively the detrimental effects of prolonged stress on our emotional and physiological well-being.

Some commonsense reasons explain this cause-and-effect relationship. For example, financial stress can lead to working long hours, which can tempt us to abandon healthy habits we typically follow. We might end up skipping exercise, losing sleep, or eating fast food as we drive home from the office at 8:00 p.m. When we forfeit proper exercise, sleep, and nutrition, we abandon three of our most potent coping strategies for managing stress and defending against burnout.

What's more, stress can prompt us to seek temporary relief in unhealthy habits that create *more* stress in the long run. Turning to alcohol, comfort food, or overspending might provide temporary relief and distraction, but eventually it complicates our lives and adds to our stress.

WHEN WE EXPERIENCE ONGOING STRESS, IT TRIGGERS DETRIMENTAL PROCESSES WITHIN OUR BODIES.

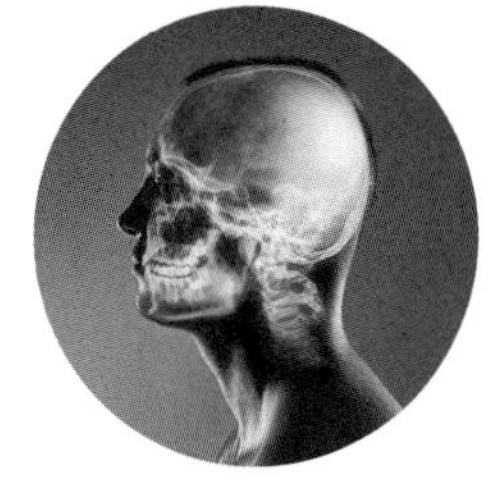

But there's much more to this dynamic than the idea that stress tempts us to abandon good habits and pursue bad ones. Science tells us that when we experience stress—particularly ongoing, chronic stress—it triggers detrimental processes within our bodies.

Researchers George Slavich and Michael Irwin examined the relationship between prolonged stress and emotional health. They observed that prolonged stress—especially stress related to interpersonal loss or rejection—triggers something called *adaptive immunity,* which increases physical inflammation not only at the sites of past trauma but also throughout the entire body. This chronic, systemic inflammation has been linked to a variety of serious diseases, including asthma, arthritis, diabetes, obesity, hardening of the arteries, cancer, Alzheimer's disease, anxiety, and depression.[9]

Whole-Person Healing

As you can see from these studies, burnout is not limited to what's happening "in your head." And it's not a condition you just need to "put up with" as an expected part of modern-day life. Far from it! Numerous factors contributed to the onset of your burnout, and each must be addressed throughout the healing process as well.

YOU WERE NOT BORN TO BARELY SURVIVE—YOU WERE BORN TO THRIVE.

In the following pages, I'll suggest a plan with six key strategies for healing your whole person. None of these practical remedies fall into the category of a "magic bullet" or "quick fix," because the truth is that it took you a long time to slide into burnout, and it will take time to recover.

But there is real hope and help available to you. The whole-person plan is a proven method that works. For forty years, I've watched as people who were desperate for help and without hope regained vitality and buoyancy after weeks, months, or years of burnout.

You were not born to barely survive—you were born to thrive. Jeremiah 29:11 states, "'I know the plans I have for you,' declares the Lord, 'plans to prosper you and not to harm you, plans to give you hope and a future.'" The Creator wanted good things for his people back then, and he still does today. The time will never be more right to begin your journey back to abundant wellness.

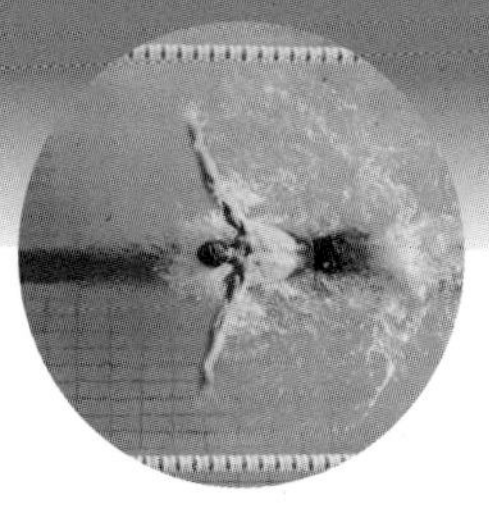

KEY 1

Streamline Your Stress

If you were to ask Keisha to describe the previous twenty years of her life, two words would come immediately to her mind: *survival mode.*

Two decades ago, Keisha was trying to survive an emotionally abusive marriage. When she finally made the decision to leave, she became enmeshed in a grueling and bitter divorce. Then came the financial stress of starting a business to support herself and her three children.

Keisha's stress continued to escalate when her ex-husband decided he needed a two-year "break" from paying child support, throwing her family into further financial disarray. Eventually Keisha hired a family-law attorney and went back to court. Thankfully the judge ruled in her favor, ordering her ex to resume paying child support and provide reimbursement for the months he didn't pay. After getting caught up on overdue bills, Keisha was able to stop foreclosure proceedings on her home with less than a month to spare.

By then, her youngest child was in his mid-teens and discovering the lure of alcohol. For three frightening years, Keisha tried desperately to get her son the help he needed. She was living on high alert while navigating the strain of his many lies and self-destructive choices.

By the time her son committed to sobriety and was tracking to become a well-adjusted young man, Keisha felt like she was taking her first deep breath in many years: Her kids were doing well. She was no longer living paycheck to paycheck. She wasn't waking up in a panic and wondering how she would get through another exhausting day.

The threats and dangers that had besieged her had subsided. She was grateful that life seemed to have leveled out—finally! Still, Keisha's burnout, fatigue, and inner turmoil did not vanish right away. In fact, she soon realized she had little optimism about the future and a lack of enthusiasm for her improved lifestyle. Instead of embracing this new season with joy, Keisha felt herself disengaging from everyone around her. As her isolation grew, she battled increasingly negative thoughts, and her emotions continued their steady decline into what felt like an abyss of sadness.

Thankfully, Keisha reached the point where she knew she needed help. A friend recommended a therapist, and Keisha took the brave step of starting regular sessions. There she found a supportive, listening ear and learned specific steps she could take to reduce the stressors in her life. Gradually she noticed that her emotions were stabilizing and her outlook brightening.

Six Strategies to Streamline Stress

Not everything that caused Keisha's stress could be eliminated, and the same is true for the rest of us. In fact, low levels of stress are actually necessary to stimulate the brain, boosting productivity and concentration. Low levels of stress can also motivate us to solve problems and accomplish goals.

THERE ARE PLENTY OF STRESSORS IN OUR LIVES THAT WE *CAN* CONTROL.

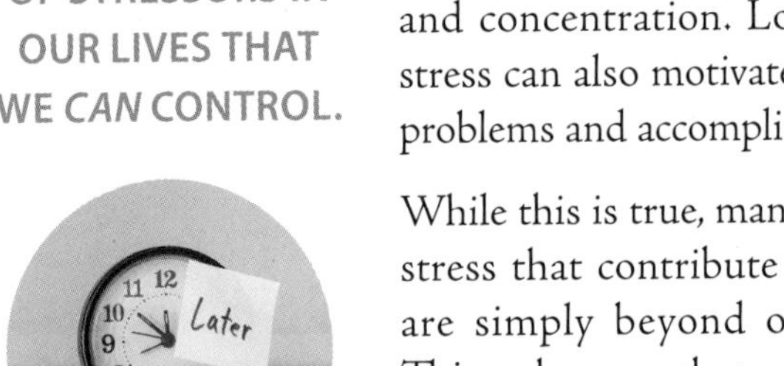

While this is true, many sources of stress that contribute to burnout are simply beyond our control. Things happen that we could not have foreseen or avoided, such as changes in the economy, an employer declaring bankruptcy, an accident or illness, and the decisions of others that leave us gravely impacted.

That said, there are still plenty of stressors in our lives that we *can* control. Indeed, eliminating them will leave us healthier and happier. Let's look at six stress-management strategies that Keisha followed—and that you can begin to practice immediately.

1 Stop Procrastinating

We all procrastinate sometimes, but for some people, procrastination is a way of life. Whether you are an occasional procrastinator or a serial procrastinator, your delays and avoidance amp up your stress levels. Naturally, the more you procrastinate when it comes to taking care of your responsibilities, the more stressed you become.

Why do we procrastinate in the first place? Procrastination expert Dr. Joseph Ferrari says there are three types of procrastinators:[10]

- Thrill seekers who get a rush out of waiting until the last minute
- Avoiders who see procrastination as a way of sidestepping something unpleasant, like criticism, failure, or even the unwanted pressure of success
- People who struggle to make a decision and want to avoid taking responsibility for the outcome of their choice

Chances are, there is something in your life that is making you feel anxious ... not because you can't change it, but because you are putting off doing what is needed to resolve that source of stress once and for all.

2 Limit Your Commitments

Something else that is largely within your control to manage is the scope of your commitments. Most of us have overflowing agendas because we're not good at saying no to new requests and opportunities. Granted, sometimes when situations impose on our lives and schedules, we can find ourselves overwhelmed as a result. If we're not careful, however, we can grow accustomed to living in a familiar state of overload and never learn to say no.

Protecting your time from commitments that are within your control to refuse may not be easy, but it's one of the most effective things you can do to reduce stress in your life. Learn the fine art of gracefully declining by saying, "That sounds wonderful, but unfortunately I just can't accept at this time."

3 Forgo Escapes That Increase Your Stress

Taking a mental and emotional break from whatever is overwhelming you is a powerful tool that can improve how you cope, transform your perspective, and even help you identify long-term solutions. But being intentional about *how* you take needed escapes is critical, and what you choose can determine how long you stay stressed and how much damage you sustain in the process.

BEING INTENTIONAL ABOUT *HOW* YOU TAKE NEEDED ESCAPES IS CRITICAL.

When we are stressed, it's tempting to turn to unhealthy escapes that can change our mood, such as gambling, pornography, substance abuse, and excessive eating, spending, or alcohol consumption. Of course, the list could go on. But although these unhealthy and potentially destructive activities may help us temporarily forget about the stress in our lives, the ramifications will eventually leave us more stressed than ever.

4 Embrace Healthy Escapes

A healthy escape could range from reading a good book while lounging in a backyard hammock to getting away for a weekend or more in a faraway location.

If you choose to stay local, how about spending an afternoon at the zoo or going to a local park or forest preserve? Taking a walk in nature is an escape that is good for your body, emotions, and brain. Watching a favorite comedy is another escape that won't complicate your life or add to your stress after the credits roll.

Another option is to explore something new. For example, drive around a part of town you're unacquainted with, or go to your favorite coffee shop and order a menu item you've never tried before.

Since all of us are created uniquely, we each require different ways to rejuvenate ourselves. Extroverts get recharged by being around other people. Introverts get recharged by walking quietly in the woods or curling up with a good book. Creative people may need to regularly attend the symphony or art gallery. Nature lovers need to go hiking or work in the garden. Identify your boosters and enjoy them often.

5 Put an End to Isolation

When we're stressed, it's tempting to isolate. If we're already feeling overwhelmed, the last thing we want to do is expend energy to drive to an event or connect with a friend after work. And yet study after study shows that supportive relationships are huge factors when it comes to improving how we experience and process stress. Other studies show that people involved in faith communities tend to have lower levels of anxiety and stress because they are not only connecting with like-minded people but also feeling more connected to God.

Although it might seem taxing at first, making the effort to connect with others eases stress levels as you prioritize the importance of healthy relationships. It's interesting to note that wisdom from the Bible also backs this up: "Two are better than one, because they have a good return for their labor: If either of them falls down, one can help the other up. But pity anyone who falls and has no one to help them up" (Ecclesiastes 4:9–10).

6 Guard Your Thoughts

Thinking about negative or painful experiences, refusing to forgive, and having a negative outlook on life create ongoing stress. We all have an inner voice that tries to forecast a dismal future by replaying our faults, failures, inadequacies, and unfortunate experiences. But we also control the on-off switch for that voice. Refuse to sit still for self-inflicted verbal beatings any longer. Shut off the flow of negative messages coming into your brain and redirect your thoughts to uplifting memories. Choose to accept your shortcomings and celebrate your strengths.

■ ■ ■

Think back on Keisha's burnout experience. The stress she endured over the course of two decades came from a variety of sources, both within her control and beyond it. As she learned healthy ways to manage current stressors, she slowly moved beyond her deep exhaustion, pain, and sadness.

WHEN WE LEARN TO MANAGE OUR STRESS, WE'RE WELL ON OUR WAY TO HEALING FROM BURNOUT.

For each of us, it's impossible to eliminate all stress from our lives. But how much stress we experience—and how we respond to it—are largely in our control. And when we learn to manage our stress, we're well on our way to healing from burnout.

BURNOUT BUSTERS

1. **Make a list of the factors contributing to your stress.** For now, focus on addressing only one or two. These might include:
   - Stressors you could eliminate if you stopped procrastinating
   - Overcommitment issues
   - Unhealthy habits you use to escape or avoid dealing with issues
   - Isolation tendencies
   - Unhealthy thought patterns
2. **Identify a partner who can provide accountability and encouragement.** You're not the only one who is stressed. Ask someone you know to join you on this journey. Brainstorm fun stress-busting activities together, hold each other accountable, and celebrate each other's successes.
3. **Evaluate your inner voice.** Tonight before bed, take a few minutes to ponder the quality of your thoughts throughout the day. Were they generally positive and productive? Critical and judgmental? Think of some specific ways you can make your thoughts an ally, not an enemy, of your well-being.

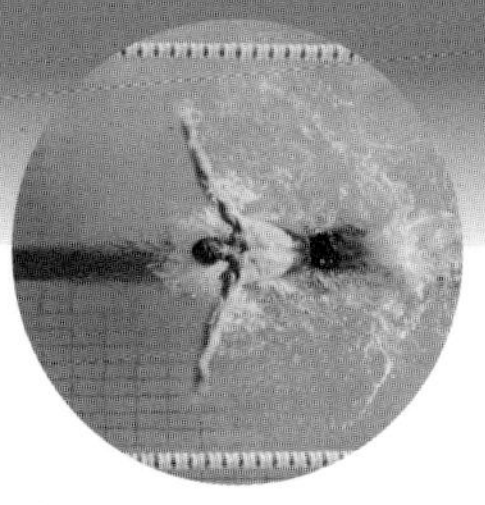

KEY 2

Reclaim Your True Self

"*I've lost* touch with the things that used to help me feel alive and energized. In fact, I've lost my true self—who I am down deep in my heart and soul. Why am I doing all of this and running myself ragged? I've become a 'human doing' instead of a 'human being.'"

That honest admission came from Maya, the owner of a small café my wife and I have frequented over several years. She went on to describe the pressure bearing down on her as she performed the duties of a small-business owner: paying bills, managing inventory, repairing equipment, opening the shop at dawn's early light, and cleaning after closing.

Plus she was having trouble finding reliable employees.

Plus business was down after customers discovered the trendy chain bistro that opened around the corner.

Plus she was a single parent raising a fifteen-year-old daughter. Sadly, her husband died in a construction accident several years before. If anyone was a prime candidate for burnout, it was Maya.

"Many days, I just want to climb into bed, pull the covers up, and sleep for an entire week. But I've got a business to run by myself and a teenager to care for."

Maya paused to compose herself when tears formed in her eyes. Then she continued, saying, "I used to have a grand plan for my life, a dream of what I wanted to accomplish for myself and my family. Now I just wonder why I'm doing all of this. I'm ready to give up."

Getting to Know You

You can likely relate to Maya's heartfelt comments, though your circumstances are probably different. You know the pain. You know the struggle to press on. You know the desperation.

Maya used the phrase "I've lost my true self." I have heard that description, in various words, from numerous friends and clients struggling with burnout. Most of them struggle with a sense of being lost, derailed from their dreams and detached from the people and activities once important to them. Feeling worn down for an extended time can cause them to question their purpose in life, their abilities, and their future. Therefore, an essential part of burnout recovery is regaining a sense of your true self—understanding who you are and where you want to go.

AN ESSENTIAL PART OF BURNOUT RECOVERY IS UNDERSTANDING WHO YOU ARE AND WHERE YOU WANT TO GO.

With these challenges in mind, let's explore five ways you can actively become reacquainted with the person you have lost touch with as burnout has overtaken you.

1 Focus on What You Do Best

While working through burnout, you might feel a bit disoriented about where you're headed, and that's okay. Even if you feel "wobbly," in time you will regain your steadiness. In the aftermath of burnout, you can build resilience one small step at a time by returning to and concentrating on what you do best and enjoy the most.

Perhaps it's time to take a fresh look at the skills, experiences, and partnerships that you've already built and the successes you've achieved, both professionally and personally. In other words, play to your strengths. Let's say the boss wants the final sales report on her desk in twenty-four hours. If you're not great on compiling the data but are awesome on layout, go for the design and try to find someone else who can run the numbers.

Think about it: Even the world's most elite Olympic athletes don't compete in several different sports. A highly focused sprinter doesn't also take on boxing, water polo, and fencing. The athlete must train and aim for gold in his or her *best* sport.

2 Prevail over Perfectionism

We all admire people who strive to be their best, maximize their potential, and pursue big achievements. But for many, the quest for excellence crosses the line into obsessively trying to perform flawlessly. One definition states that a perfectionist is "a person who refuses to accept any standard other than flawlessness and regards anything less as a failure."

It's no surprise, then, that the majority of burned-out people also have a perfectionistic streak. After all, perfectionism can often breed guilt, anxiety, depression, sleep problems, and low self-esteem—damaging conditions associated with burnout.

As stated by Julia Cameron, best-selling author of *The Artist's Way*, "Perfectionism is not a quest for the best. It is a pursuit of the worst in ourselves, the part that tells us that nothing we do will ever be good enough—that we should try again."[11]

This is why self-acceptance is so essential. The key to contented and balanced living is the recognition that perfection is never the standard for having worth and value. Accept your shortcomings, and realize that everyone has areas that need work. No person's self-worth is determined by their degree of perfection or imperfection.

Reclaim your true self by finally admitting that you can't do it all flawlessly. What a relief!

3 Clarify What Counts as Guilt

When you're burned out, you often feel guilty, even when you've done nothing wrong. This leaves you emotionally confused. Your conscience is prone to questioning your motives or chastising yourself for things you haven't done. You berate yourself for not "keeping it together" or failing to live up to your own or someone else's ideals. Often false guilt is closely tied to a fear of disapproval from others.

FALSE GUILT IS CLOSELY TIED TO A FEAR OF DISAPPROVAL FROM OTHERS.

A sense of healthy guilt, however, helps redirect your course when you've truly made an error and need to ask for forgiveness. Part of regaining your footing after burnout is knowing where you stand with false guilt and healthy guilt. Here's one simple question to ask yourself: *Do I have a legitimate reason for feeling guilty about this situation, or am I believing lies?* Your honest answer and counsel from trusted friends will help you wisely discern what counts as true guilt.

4 Change Your Thought Channel

When your tank is empty after running on overdrive, it can seem like the world has it out for you. Your thoughts may sound like a streaming app set on repeat:

- *I never catch a break. Nothing ever turns out in my favor.*
- *No one really cares about me. I always have to look out for myself.*

Your thoughts can quickly send you spiraling downward into self-pity and depression. And that's truly unfortunate, because broad "woe is me" statements are rarely true. According to psychiatrist Neel Burton,

> People with low self-esteem tend to see the world as a hostile place and themselves as its victim. As a result, they are reluctant to express and assert themselves, miss out on experiences and opportunities, and feel powerless to change things. All this lowers their self-esteem still further, sucking them into a downward spiral.[12]

It's important to change your negative thought channel by giving yourself a mental fact-check. Remember the good things that have happened: Did you receive a good health report from your doctor? Pay your bills on time?

Enjoy quality time with your loved ones? Make it a habit to mine your thoughts for the positives in life.

5 See Yourself as God Sees You

You are a one-of-a-kind reflection of God's image, whether you realize it or not. God designed you with fathomless creativity and enduring emotional tenacity. Artificial Intelligence could never come close to imitating the masterpiece that you are! As you recover from burnout and rebuild balance in your life, it's crucial to align your view of yourself with God's view. God doesn't need corrective lenses. His eyesight is infinitely beyond perfect. Through Jesus Christ, he sees you as blessed, chosen, holy, blameless, loved, adopted, accepted, redeemed, forgiven, wise, and so much more (Ephesians 1:3–8). Day by day, as you practice seeing yourself the way that God sees you, you are strengthening your spiritual and emotional resilience.

■ ■ ■

Earlier I told you about Maya, the café owner and single parent facing extreme burnout—and struggling to reclaim her true self. In time she realized she needed to make major lifestyle changes that included many of the steps in this chapter:

- She focused on her strengths and recognized that performing perfectly in every area of her life was not only impossible but also toxic.
- She recognized how the difficulties in her life had been a breeding ground for false guilt.
- She realized she had the power to resist negative thoughts, and she accepted that her circumstances did not dictate her identity.
- She embraced God's truth about her incredible worth, giving her peace for the present and hope for the future.

In time, these changes strengthened Maya's confidence in her true self, the Maya that God created and loves. Operating from this fresh awareness, Maya decided to shorten the hours her café stayed open each day, took an entire day off each week for self-renewal, and asked family members to pitch in a few hours each week to help with duties at home and the café.

These were all positive steps toward healing, though Maya knows that recovery from burnout takes careful lifestyle monitoring over a long period. But Maya is well on her way to reclaiming her true self and the dreams she once had.

BURNOUT BUSTERS

1. **Think about how burnout has been a positive part of your journey.** This might sound absurd when you're in the depths of burnout. But reflecting on the recovery process might help you rediscover what you've lost sight of along the way—your passions, dreams, and God-given strengths.

2. **Focus on what you're good at.** Engage your strengths by participating in at least one activity that leaves you feeling empowered.

3. **Identify one distorted thought and replace it with the truth.** Write out self-critical thoughts that come to mind. Choose one and replace it with a positive truth. For instance, exchange *I'm a failure* with *God made me in his image. He has a specific purpose for me that is good*.

4. **Read the Bible.** The Bible is a written record of the quest that leads us back to our true selves—and to a loving, nurturing, healing God.

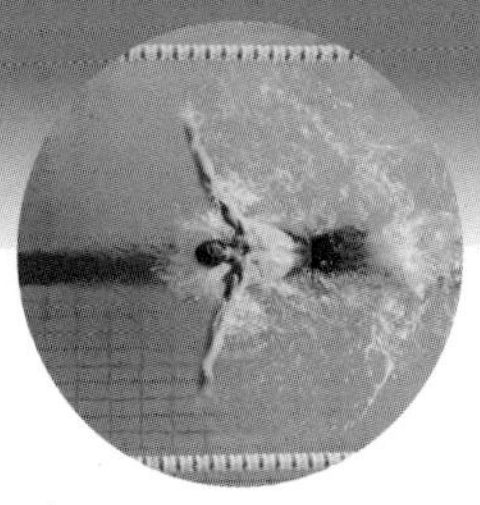

KEY 3

Find Sanity through Simplicity

In 2014, a little book with an odd title made a big splash in the publishing world and popular culture. *The Life-Changing Magic of Tidying Up* was on best-seller lists for multiple weeks and has since sold millions of copies. Written by Marie Kondo, a Japanese organizing consultant, the key concept is to shed everything you own that does not "spark joy." Discard possessions that do not bring you delight, and you will enjoy a peaceful living space.

With follow-up books and a popular Netflix series, Marie Kondo started a global movement toward embracing simplicity and finding joy in the things we own and the way we live. Obviously, the author's message struck a massive chord. Why? Because millions of people are seeking sanity through simplicity! I have never met Marie Kondo, but I'd love to. Her crusade toward simplified living aligns perfectly with my approach toward mental health and wellness. I have seen countless times that a life out of balance—too much stuff, too many obligations, too much stress—leads to all kinds of mental health issues. Including burnout.

There's More to Clutter than Stuff

Numerous studies have shown a consistent link between material clutter and burnout, depression, and anxiety. Researchers have recognized that a cluttered, chaotic environment and emotional problems often form a destructive feedback loop, each worsening the other.

Unfortunately, however, simplicity is not just about holding a yard sale and getting rid of your surplus junk. That's a part of the program, for sure, and a big part at that. But it's important to keep in mind that decluttering your physical surroundings is not the end of the story when it comes to moving beyond burnout.

When I met Martin, he'd been living in a tent for nearly a year after working as a software engineer for a rising tech company in California's Silicon Valley. He'd given up a six-figure income and a nice home in a trendy neighborhood, filled with every convenience.

Although Martin had practically been guaranteed a secure future, he was also, as he put it, "slowly choking to death." He felt strangled by endless pressure at work and the fatigue of sitting in traffic for hours as he commuted.

At work, he was well-known for having an office with a "filing system" that only he understood. At home, his counters were cluttered with tech magazines and manuals, as well as dozens of gadgets he'd bought online—many of them still unopened. Unwashed laundry and dirty dishes littered every room.

DECLUTTERING YOUR PHYSICAL SURROUNDINGS IS NOT THE END OF THE STORY.

"Finally, I snapped," he admitted. "In one flash of insight, I saw myself as a whale covered in barnacles, and I was sinking."

Martin quit his job and moved "off the grid." As far off as he could. He bought a tiny tent and pitched it deep in the forest north of San Francisco. He sold or gave away everything he owned, trimming his possessions to only what was essential for survival. Martin lived the escapist fantasy of most burned-out people: Run away and be freed from endless obligations and demands.

"I was looking for peace," he recalled. "I needed a reset button I could press on modern life."

For a while, it worked. He could breathe again. He enjoyed doing things with his hands and feeling closer to nature. He loved leaving the relentless pressures of work far behind.

And then that season passed.

"I suddenly found myself sitting by the fire at night, reliving every lousy moment I'd ever experienced," Martin said. "All my broken relationships followed me like ghosts, along with all the same fears I'd had before. And now I also worried about forest fires or being discovered by a ranger or eaten by a bear. And what if I had a medical emergency? On and on it went."

In his haste to simplify his life, Martin had failed to understand that clutter comes in many forms—most of it unaffected by yard sales or bonfires. He learned that it takes an entirely different kind of broom to clean out our mental and emotional attics. Fortunately, Martin eventually found the help he needed.

Besides getting rid of the clutter that crowds your surrounding physical space, consider the following five actions to gain the upper hand on burnout.

1 Declutter Your Thoughts

In today's world, we are dependent on technologies that few of us understand. They're also far removed from our daily experience: for example, satellites in space, quantum computers, and the mysterious workings of the stock market.

Before finishing our morning coffee, we know the latest information about everything from wars on other continents to fashion trends in Europe. We look up the weather forecast, plan the next family reunion, study the latest political polls—on and on it goes. Most of what occupies our minds is utterly beyond our control and will have no effect on the day ahead.

Here's the secret I want you to grasp: You have the power to *choose* what occupies your mind. You can decide to displace the clutter with thoughts that inspire confidence and faith. Give yourself permission to *not* know everything for a change, and you'll be astonished to learn how good that feels.

2 Declutter Your Emotions

Do you struggle with forgiving offenses you've suffered at the hands of others? Or perhaps you harbor crippling regret over something you did to harm someone. Both situations are often accompanied by the fear you'll never find your way to peace and freedom—which is yet another factor that can lead to burnout. Once again, the good news is that you are not simply stuck in the emotional traps life has laid in your path. You can choose what to feel and how you'll respond to emotional challenges.

The apostle Paul wrote, "Three things will last forever—faith, hope, and love—and the greatest of these is love" (1 Corinthians 13:13 NLT). Declaring this, he offered a clear alternative to being enslaved by toxic emotions. Actively—even aggressively—pursue faith, hope, and love as your chosen way of being. This is not about denying your wounds or your mistakes; it's about taming their pain so you can move forward and repair what's broken. One of the clearest roadmaps ever drawn for how to get there is contained in Reinhold Niebuhr's Serenity Prayer:

God, grant me the serenity to
accept the things I cannot change,

Courage to change the things I can,

And the wisdom to know
the difference.

In these few words, we are offered permission to let go of what is beyond our control or was never ours to carry in the first place. It's a call to action—to bravely do what we can—but also an acknowledgment that we need help in sorting out how to succeed.

3 Declutter Your Relationships

It's true that each of us needs to take personal responsibility for the problems we face and own any part we may have played. But it's also true that other people sometimes cause or contribute to the problems we face. Toxic people exist, and often they play a role in our downward spiral into burnout.

ACTIVELY PURSUE FAITH, HOPE, AND LOVE AS YOUR CHOSEN WAY OF BEING.

When you sense that someone is not good for you, it can be difficult to know whether you should stay away from them completely or simply limit your exposure by constructing healthy boundaries.

Here's a litmus test that might help: Answer the question, *How do I feel after being around [name] for any period of time?* If you feel empowered, uplifted, and enriched—good! This is a relationship you can nourish. But if you consistently feel depleted, degraded, or depressed, then it's better to let go.

On your journey from burnout to wellness, you need all the help you can get. People who function like emotional deadweight are not your friends, no matter how conditioned you are to think of them that way.

It's not easy to make changes to relationships that have been part of your life for a long time. Once you start setting and holding boundaries, you may find that troublesome people wander off on their own. It's also possible they may surprise you by moving into action to give you what you need. Either way, you win.

4 Declutter Your Goals

"There's no heavier burden than a great potential." This sentiment is more true today than when the beloved *Peanuts* character Linus uttered these fateful words (with the help of legendary cartoonist Charles Schulz).[13] That's because the digital-information age has granted us access to opportunity like never before.

The message of the American Dream is that you can become anything you choose, and it has never been louder or more convincing. But it can deliver an unintended message as well: If you haven't "succeeded" (as defined by popular culture), it's your own fault.

However, the truth for some people is that just getting by is a constant battle. It's hard enough to pay the rent on time and put food on the table, no matter how many opportunities for advancement exist. The painfully obvious difference between this reality and the common notion of "success" can place a heavy burden of guilt on low-income people. Even those who have a rewarding career and material prosperity can easily feel a sense of failure at not having achieved more.

LET GO OF GOALS THAT DON'T ADD VALUE TO YOUR LIFE.

By now it's likely that you know what the solution is for avoiding this detrimental source of stress and anxiety: *Exercise your power to choose for yourself what goals you invest in, and let go of those that don't add a sense of value to your life.* Make your gift of potential serve you—not the other way around.

5 Declutter Your Time

Life is full of people, obligations, and tasks that siphon off our energy. If you follow the advice you've read so far, you are guaranteed to reap a reward in reclaimed time.

You'll spend fewer hours caught in a fog of cluttered thoughts and emotions. You'll give less precious time to people who take and never give back.

Still, the problem of cluttered time deserves attention all its own. Of all the sources of stress and anxiety in modern life, the feeling that there is too much to do and not enough time to do it tops the list. Deadlines and appointments can feel like a pack of wolves snarling at your heels from dawn to dusk.

Much of this is non-negotiable—grocery shopping, parent-teacher conferences, medical appointments, and professional obligations. But if we're honest, we'll agree it's the optional things that consume the most time: television, social media, web surfing, recreational shopping, bingeing on YouTube videos.

In proper proportion, there's nothing wrong with any of these. While you're in a simplifying mood, however, take a hard look at where your time goes. Freeing up a couple of hours a day can go a long way toward silencing the hounds—and moving beyond burnout.

■ ■ ■

These days, lots of people dream of getting out of the "fast lane" and living life more deliberately, more simply. Some succeed in finding that breathing room, and many don't. For people who are struggling to overcome burnout, however, this goal is no longer optional. Simplicity is powerful medicine and should be a key part of their healing plan.

It seems only right for decluttering expert Marie Kondo to have the final word with this parting bit of encouragement: "**Keep only those things that speak to your heart. Then take the plunge and discard all the rest.** By doing this, you can reset your life and embark on a new lifestyle."[14]

Plunge. Discard. Reset. Embark. These are empowering words as you emerge from the darkness of burnout into the light of a decluttered, energized, and joyful life.

BURNOUT BUSTERS

1. **Have less.** Go through one room in your house and look for things that no longer have purpose or add value to your life. Commit to getting rid of at least five items—just for starters.
2. **Do less.** Next, look at your calendar. Do any of your obligations serve to simply distract you or fill time? Do they serve to fulfill someone else's idea of what you should be doing? If so, consider eliminating at least one optional or draining activity each day. For example, cut back on car trips that leave you stuck in traffic, or steer clear of people who soak up your energy.
3. **Go online less.** Studies consistently suggest a significant link between too much time online—especially on social media platforms—and elevated depression and anxiety. Take a break by powering off your devices for at least twenty-four hours.
4. **Access the news less.** As the old saying goes, "No news is good news." Abstaining from the news for a time will calm your worry over things beyond your control. Start with three days, and notice how good *not* knowing the news can feel.

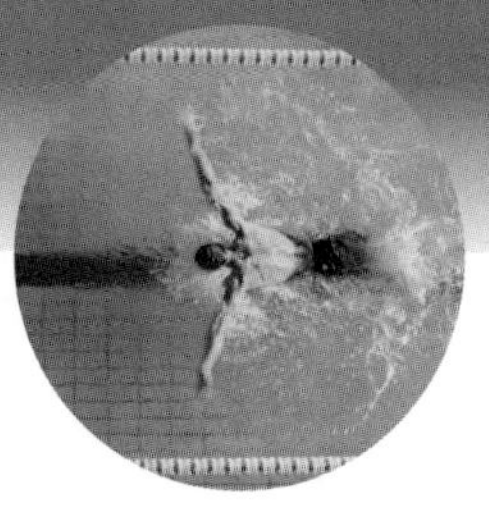

KEY 4

Bolster Your Body

What began as a mild case of burnout for John had evolved and grown significantly worse in recent years. Now in his early forties, John came to our clinic with severe depression. He was a hundred pounds overweight and rarely left his house. He also had major digestive upset and was taking multiple medications—three for depression and one for anxiety, and a variety of over-the-counter drugs to help settle his gut.

Looking for help, he'd "done it all," he told us, like so many of our clients do. But years of visits to different medical specialists left him with disjointed and ineffective care. Based on a careful review of John's files, it was clear he had received some good advice, but one question had never been asked by the assortment of practitioners he'd seen: "What's going into your mouth every day?"

Yes, he talked to more than a few doctors about his rapid weight gain and its effects. But sadly, those conversations usually went something like this:

"You know you need to lose some weight."

"Yes, I know."

"You need to eat better."

"Yeah, I know."

Round and round it went. But circling an issue means you never get to the core of the problem.

What we found during John's intake assessment shocked us. Self-employed and working from home, John was able to hide an incredible addiction: He consumed an average of twelve pots of coffee a day. Not twelve *cups*—twelve *pots*. He shared with me that no one had ever asked him how much coffee he drank, so he never thought to mention it.

All that caffeine was causing numerous issues that were directly undermining his recovery from depression. It had rinsed the B vitamins out of his system, severely upset the balance of "good" bacteria in his gut, and derailed his appetite, causing him to binge-eat large amounts of sugary foods. All of this in turn led to even more health problems.

Since coffee had become John's only fluid intake, his body also settled into a state of permanent dehydration, hindering his mental capacity and other basic bodily functions. And yet despite how horrible he felt, John was seriously dependent on the coffee. "I need it just to help me get through the day," he insisted.

Over the next few weeks, John began to rehydrate his body by drinking one bottle of water for every cup of coffee. Eventually his coffee intake dropped to three cups a day—and none after 10:00 a.m. Once a week he received an IV infusion of vitamins, minerals, and amino acids, which activated his brain chemistry. His cravings started to decrease, especially for sugar and caffeine. For the first time in years, John started eating a healthy breakfast and lunch. He steadily lost weight, and his energy levels and sense of well-being increased measurably each week.

The last time I spoke with John, he was doing remarkably better than just a year prior. He'd maintained his increased physical activity by playing tennis, a sport he had abandoned years ago when it became too difficult to leave his house. His home-based business had improved along with his mood, and he was down to one medication for depression.

John may have been an extreme case with his excessive caffeine consumption and resulting problems, but his situation points to something that many people struggling with burnout tend to overlook: the powerful connection between physical health and emotional wellness.

Overcoming Burnout's Physical Connection

Father Anthony Coniaris may have had someone like John in mind when he observed, "The truth is that the body and the soul live so close to each other that they often catch one another's sicknesses, illnesses, and diseases."[15]

I'm guessing that, like John, you've allowed the upheavals of burnout to preoccupy you, and as your mind and emotions have suffered, so has your body. Perhaps your fitness and overall health have become less of a priority. Or maybe, in spite of your best efforts to stay healthy, the strain of burnout has simply worn you down. This is why we're going to examine four strategies to help you revitalize your body so it will sustain *the whole you* as you tackle your recovery.

1 Focus on Healthy Nutrition

God created our bodies to run on proper fuel, not prepackaged foods with ingredients that are difficult to pronounce. To move beyond burnout, it's vital that you enhance the quality of fuel you put in your body by committing (or recommitting) to the following essentials of healthy nutrition.

Plenty of Filtered Water

Your body is 50 to 65 percent water, and about 50 percent of your blood is made up of water. Throughout the day, you *need* abundant amounts of water for your systems to function properly. Consuming *filtered* water is important because of the many chemicals and impurities often present in tap water. Accomplishing this can be as simple as purchasing an inexpensive filtration pitcher at your local store.

Plain water is the best source of hydration, but other drinks and high-water-content foods can help contribute to your daily water intake. It is important to choose wisely because some beverages contain high amounts of unwanted ingredients. Energy or sports drinks that contain sugar, electrolytes, or caffeine can be beneficial during exercise, but if consumed regularly, they might negatively affect other areas of your health.

If plain water seems boring, adding a slice of lemon, lime, or orange can add extra zip. And don't forget that water is also abundant in many soups, broths, and fruits and vegetables, such as watermelon, strawberries, lettuce, cucumbers, celery, and tomatoes.

How much is enough? Nutritionists suggest dividing your body weight in half and drinking that many ounces of water each day. For example, if you weigh 130 pounds, divide 130 by 2, which means that your goal is to consume 65 ounces of filtered water every day. Start by drinking two cups of filtered water each morning to rehydrate and flush out your system. Then continue drinking water throughout the day, reducing your intake a few hours before bedtime.

Fruits and Veggies

The U.S. Department of Agriculture's MyPlate.gov resource recommends an average of five servings of fresh fruits and vegetables daily for adults. The right amount of produce you should consume depends on your specific sex, age, height, weight, and physical activity. Organic foods that are locally sourced offer the least amount of exposure to chemicals, pesticides, and insecticides, and they often taste better.

Frozen produce is the next-most-healthy choice for taste and nutritional content. Canned fruits and vegetables typically lack in taste and have decreased amounts of nutrients, including vitamins A and C, magnesium, and zinc. Always read packaging, particularly for canned produce, to determine whether unhealthy amounts of salt, sugar, or preservatives have been added.

Whole Grains

We all know how tempting and easy it is to fill up on the cookies, donuts, and candy that celebrating colleagues or grateful clients drop by the workplace. These delectable treats taste good at first, but soon they start dragging down energy levels, both physically and mentally.

Instead of turning to these high-carb confections that end up on your waistline, allow yourself to indulge in the healthy whole-grain fuels your body actually craves. Shift from highly processed, nutrition-free choices—sweets, white breads, plain bagels, and sugary cereals—to hearty whole-grain breads, steel-cut oatmeal, quinoa, millet, and brown rice.

Lean Protein and Healthy Fats

Lean meats and fish, eggs, and low-fat dairy products are also important sources of essential fuel. Avoid consuming *unhealthy fats* by grilling or baking meat and fish instead of frying. To increase your intake of *healthy fats*, consume more fish, as well as unprocessed, unsalted nuts and seeds, such as raw almonds, pistachios, walnuts, cashews, and sunflower seeds. Eggs, when eaten in moderation, are good sources of energy, healthy protein, and other nutrients. And despite popular misinformation from past years, a few eggs per day will not tip the cholesterol scales.

MULTIVITAMINS PROVIDE BALANCED NUTRITION WHILE TAKING THE GUESSWORK OUT OF MENU-PLANNING.

Excellent protein sources for vegetarians include plant-based foods such as soybeans, kidney beans, lima beans, black beans, fava beans, garbanzo beans, lentils, and chickpeas. Nuts and seeds—including almonds, peanuts, cashews, pecans, hazelnuts, walnuts, pumpkin seeds, sunflower seeds, and sesame seeds—are also popular sources of protein and healthy fats for those who eat a meatless diet.

Nutritional Supplements

Consulting with your physician, dietician, or nutritionist is a sound way to ensure you are balancing your body with sufficient levels of vitamins, minerals, and amino acids. None of us have the time or capacity to know whether our diet is providing the recommended daily allowance of vitamins A, B, C, D, E, and K—let alone proper amounts of selenium, calcium, magnesium, zinc, and essential amino acids. A top-quality multivitamin supplement conveniently provides balanced nutrition while taking the guesswork out of menu-planning.

2 Take Time for a Gut Check

Research has demonstrated a link between mental health and "gut," or digestive, health. Microorganisms in your digestive tract affect everything from digestive health to heart function to the immune system. They also have an impact on the brain, influencing levels of anxiety, depression, happiness, and satisfaction. Adding certain good bacteria to the gut can actually relieve stress and anxiety by lessening the production of cortisol.[16]

Prebiotics and *probiotics* are keys to a healthy gut microbiome. Prebiotics support the growth of certain healthy microorganisms, while probiotics are made up of the microorganisms themselves. *Prebiotics* pave the way for probiotics to work. They are not microorganisms—they are nutrients that help good bacteria grow and flourish. Most prebiotics are fibers or carbohydrates that can be taken as supplements or found naturally in foods.

Some examples of healthy foods and beverages that contain *probiotics* include unsweetened yogurt, kombucha, kefir, and sauerkraut. These offer billions of healthy microorganisms to help you restore and maintain gut balance. You can also find good probiotics in capsules, tablets, powders, and liquids at a grocery or health food store.

3 Get Moving

Countless studies show that regular physical movement strengthens bones and muscles, reduces unhealthy fat, and reenergizes the body. It also increases the production of natural chemicals such as *serotonin,* a mood stabilizer; *norepinephrine,* which sharpens focus and memory; and *dopamine,* which enhances pleasure and motivation. The most noticeable mood benefit occurs with the release of *endorphins*—"feel good" chemicals that aid in promoting happiness and soothing pain.

According to scientific studies, a mere five minutes of aerobic exercise can help curb anxiety. Additional research demonstrates that regular exercise is as effective as medication when it comes to reducing anxiety symptoms. One session of intense physical motion can help symptoms for hours, and according to experts, "a regular schedule may significantly reduce them over time."[17] For some people, however, medication is still needed to help regulate biochemical levels in their body. You should never change or stop taking a medication without first speaking with your physician.

Begin Slowly

When you take up the charge to get moving, be encouraged that there's no need to purchase fancy fitness clothing. Nor do you need to use expensive weights or machines or spend hours at a fitness center or with a personal trainer. Instead, consider taking the following simple actions that will allow you to begin slowly:

- Park your car farther out when you arrive at work or stop at the store.
- Take short walks outside during breaks at work.
- Opt for the stairs instead of the elevator or escalator.
- While watching your favorite shows, do a few push-ups, squats, or crunches during commercials.

Basic physical movement that stimulates your heart and lungs will increase circulation, bringing oxygen to your cells and producing chemicals that leave you relaxed and energized.

Increase Gradually

Consider your current physical stamina as you work toward better conditioning. The following suggested guidelines from the U.S. Department of Health and Human Services will allow you to gradually increase your activity levels for even better fitness:[18]

- **Moderate to intense aerobic activity** (brisk walking, running, cycling, stairs, or elliptical) for 2.5 hours per week. This is roughly 30 minutes five days per week, or 45–50 minutes per day, three days each week. The key is to move more and sit less on a consistent basis throughout the week.

- **Muscle-strengthening activities** two days each week, with the goal of working your major muscle groups (legs, core, back, chest, arms, and shoulders). One idea is to start with stretchy resistance bands and eventually advance to free weights or weight machines.

During your sessions, you will gently and safely exercise underused joints and muscles. Work just hard enough to increase your heart rate and breathe deeper. Then add both time and resistance to build your fitness level.

4 Prioritize Sleep

A broad three-year study of over nine thousand Americans found that sleep deprivation likely affects almost half of Americans adults.[19] You may be one of them, especially if you've been struggling with burnout.

When you finally fall into bed after a full day of endless tasks, it's difficult for your mind and body to wind down peacefully. Carrying stress from the day into the night means that your sleep suffers. The next day, your ability to function is negatively affected, continuing the vicious cycle.

To recover from burnout, your body, mind, and emotions need the rejuvenation and strength that come from restful sleep. Consider the following helpful tips, and note they are not limited just to bedtime.

Daytime

- **Soak up some rays.** Sunlight helps you maintain a healthy sleep cycle. Your internal clock depends on receiving intervals of light and darkness during a twenty-four-hour period. Try to take at least one fifteen-minute walk outdoors every day.
- **Exercise on purpose.** The intentional physical movement discussed earlier not only helps relieve stress but also benefits your sleep. Deep breathing and exertion help relax your mind and muscles.
- **Go easy on caffeine and alcohol.** Both beverages can increase your heart rate and blood pressure, so limit them. Let moderation be your goal, especially at night.
- **Enjoy short naps.** Some health experts advise against all napping, while others recommend short naps as needed. I encourage you to catch up on sleep any time you can. A brief nap of thirty minutes or less can reduce tension and improve mood.

Nighttime

- **Follow a relaxing bedtime routine.** A regular bedtime routine notifies your body and mind that it's time for sleep. Around the same time each evening, shift toward rest with one or more of the following activities: Take a shower or enjoy a candlelit bath; read a novel, the Bible, or an inspirational book; listen to soothing music; or practice slow, deep breathing to put you in a relaxed state.
- **Ensure a sleep-friendly atmosphere.** Invest in a top-quality mattress, and keep your bedroom at a comfortable temperature. Darken the room by shading your windows and eliminating light pollution from electronics. Relaxing music, a fan, or earplugs and eyeshades may also be beneficial. If your pets disturb you during the night, consider relocating them to another room.
- **Resist using electronics.** You want your brain to associate bedtime and your bedroom with sleepiness, not wakefulness. I recommend refraining from television and computer use in the bedroom, as well as keeping your cell phone in a different room (or at least not next to your bed). Silence your phone so you aren't awakened by incoming calls, notifications, or messages during

the night. If you wake up, resist the inclination to watch TV or check social media. These actions will confuse your internal clock and stimulate your brain. Instead, keep the room dark and practice slow, deep breathing to relax. If you're unable to fall back asleep within ten minutes, get out of bed and sit in a chair, in the dark, until you feel sleepy. Then return to bed.

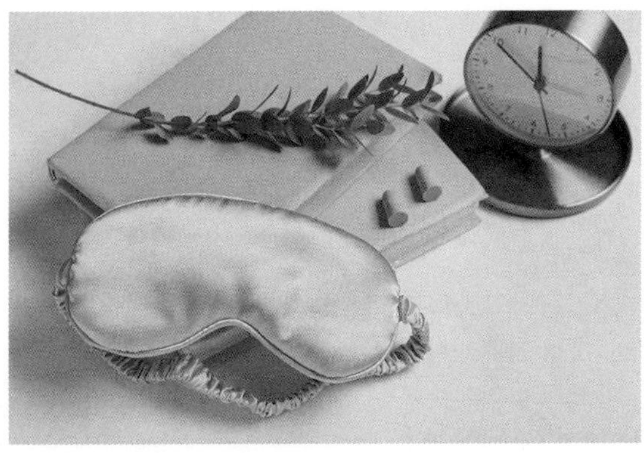

BURNOUT BUSTERS

1. **Make a specific plan to improve your diet.** Select one recommendation from strategy 1, "Focus on Healthy Nutrition," that you're determined to start today.
2. **Explore the best types of prebiotics and probiotics.** Research credible websites—or better yet, talk with a qualified nutritionist.
3. **If you've been physically inactive, determine to reverse the trend.** Before the week is over, do at least one of the simple activities suggested in the "Begin Slowly" section of strategy 3, "Get Moving."
4. **Identify two habits that may be preventing quality sleep.** Too much caffeine? Too much screen time before bed? What recommendation(s) from strategy 4, "Prioritize Sleep," can you start tonight?

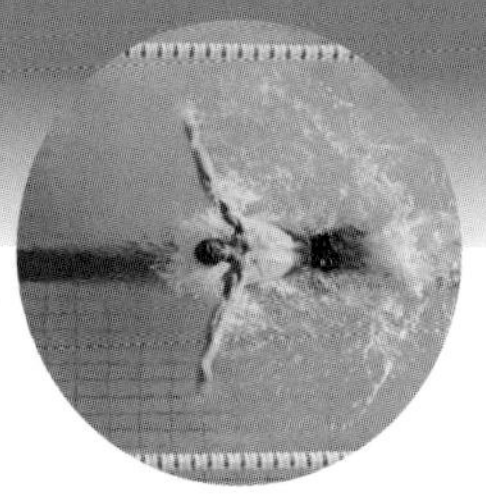

KEY 5

Fortify Your Filters

Burnout can be fueled by a broad range of influences in our lives. As we've already discussed, our own choices and behaviors often contribute to burnout. Sometimes we don't hold firm boundaries when deadlines are unreasonable or extra work is unwarranted. And sometimes we overcommit to unnecessary activities and later regret it.

But other factors can also contribute to burnout, coming from sources that we don't actively choose—for example, negative people, negative media input, and negative self-talk. The truth is that we are bombarded with detrimental messages from every direction on a daily basis.

But this doesn't mean we are helpless or handcuffed in our ability to manage what increases our stress levels and darkens our moods. Equipped with helpful information and a determination to fend off these messages, we can fortify our minds against them.

Let's take a closer look at why we need to be mindful and intentional about filtering three potential sources of negative messaging:

- The people who surround us
- The information and entertainment we access
- Our own self-talk

Sources of Negative Messaging

1 Negative Messages from Negative People

Some people in our lives build us up with encouragement, affirmation, and validation. Others do just the opposite. Parents, bosses, neighbors, and spouses can communicate negative messages that shake our confidence and cause us to question ourselves. Often we're left feeling hurt, angry, or anxious.

Leslie, age thirty, lives under the weight of constant disapproval from her aging mother. Leslie still visits her mother every week and stays in touch by phone most other days. But no matter how hard Leslie tries to please her mother, nothing she does ever seems to be good enough. Her mother inevitably responds with complaints and criticism. After every interaction, Leslie feels anxious and unsettled. Even on days they have no contact, Leslie finds it hard to keep her brain from replaying her mom's critical comments.

Or consider Dan, age twenty-nine, who says that interacting on social media increases his stress. Dan's example demonstrates that we don't have to experience a close connection with someone for their negativity to impact our mood, self-esteem, and peace of mind.

Dan says, "After I post a thought, I find myself waiting anxiously for responses, nervous that someone may disagree or even attack me over what I've shared. And I don't even post or repost controversial stuff. I'm just sharing an idea or opinion. People seem more free today than ever to slam and dump on other people." Dan makes a strong point—and he, of course, is not alone in noting that social media definitely has its drawbacks in addition to its benefits.

Like Dan, it's probable that you have felt uneasy for hours after someone added a critical comment to one of your social media posts. In fact, studies show that nearly half of middle school and high school students and four out of ten adults report being bullied online.[20] Can these negative messages increase feelings of burnout, depression, and anxiety? You bet they can.

2 Negative Messages Streamed Nonstop

As mentioned in chapter 3, information overload is another source of negative messaging that adds to our burnout. Through television and our ever-present computers and handheld devices, we are exposed to a never-ending stream of messages from the news and social media.

THERE IS A FINE LINE BETWEEN REMAINING APPROPRIATELY INFORMED AND BEING INUNDATED WITH BAD NEWS.

Political scandals, demands for social causes, rants about trending news topics, acts of violence from every corner of the globe, news of a friend's layoff, updates on the cancer treatments of a friend of a friend—all these and more stir up anxiety in both their content and incessant quantity. There is a fine line between remaining informed so we can act appropriately and being inundated with bad news that is outside the scope of our influence.

Even good news shared on social media can create anxiety or dampen our mood. An acquaintance is on a blissful cruise—again. A friend got another promotion. Someone else is celebrating the loss of forty pounds. A neighbor is expecting baby number four. If you are reading posts like these and feel overworked or unappreciated at your job, or if you're struggling to manage your weight or have been grieving infertility or the loss of a child—these happy posts can send you spiraling into an insecure place.

3 Negative Messages We Tell Ourselves

There is yet another source of negative messages—ourselves. Unfortunately, we are more than capable of adding to the influx of negativity with our own self-talk. Sometimes, as in the case of Leslie with her mom, we repeat to ourselves the negative messages we've been told by others. In other cases, the negative messages we tell ourselves come from our interpretation of experiences, events, and interactions with others. A comment that wasn't intended to hurt can be misunderstood, and suddenly we have new fodder for damaging self-talk:

- "My family doesn't appreciate all I do for them."
- "I always disappoint my friends."
- "I'm an outsider in my workplace."
- "I'll never do my job right."

- "I deserve the pain in my life."
- "I'm broken and I'll never be whole again."

The list of negative messages we tell ourselves is endless. Each one can play a huge role in worsening our burnout and inhibiting our recovery. But when it comes to reducing emotional burnout from negative messaging, you are not without options. Consider the following four strategies for filtering out the harmful messages coming into your life.

Filters for Negative Messaging

1 Realize You've Got the Power

First, know that you are capable of handling messages in a healthy, helpful manner. You don't have to continue living at the mercy of every message that comes into your life. Adopting an "I'm in charge" attitude is extremely significant for dealing with burnout. With it, you'll be prepared to take the three steps that follow this one. Without it, you'll continue to feel helpless to stop the barrage, and escaping the tension will seem hopeless.

Roger is someone who struggles with burnout, and on many days, he feels besieged by the messages that come into his life. Emails, overbearing clients, bad news from his accountant, and stress-inducing headlines and social media posts leave him feeling overwhelmed.

One day, feeling anxious and depressed, Roger decided to leave his office and take a walk around the block. While strolling, he tried something new. He gave himself a pep talk that went something like this:

> I'm in charge of my day. I'm in charge of my schedule. I'm in charge of my attitude. I don't have to live my life reacting to everything that comes my way. I can choose to meet deadlines so I have happier clients and less stress. I can choose to block out times in my calendar to plan or think. I get to choose my responses to everything that comes my way.

By the time Roger returned to his desk, his anxiety had been replaced with new direction and energy. He hadn't yet taken any actions or made any practical changes, but his shift in mindset and perspective was a game-changer. Recognizing that he has more control in his life than he once thought has been empowering. It has also positively influenced the way he thinks about himself, the events of his day, and his overall life.

2 Reduce the Noise

With the right mindset in place, now it's time to take steps to filter out some of the noise. What follows are a few practical suggestions:

- **Don't let social media be your go-to break.** Amid your busy, productive day, it's natural and healthy to take an occasional breather. During those times, it's all too easy to turn to social media. Instead, consider taking a walk, making a cup of tea, calling a friend, lifting weights, catching up on your latest read, or listening to uplifting music.
- **Unfollow negative people on social media.** When you do make occasional time for social media, remember that you have control over the information you allow into your life. Use the content options in your social media account to screen out negative messaging.
- **Turn off notifications on your phone.** You'll be less distracted by new posts and messages if you aren't being notified continually.
- **Use your phone to set boundaries on its use.** Most phones allow you to set limits on your screen time. Employing this feature will help silence the noise.

- **Consider a full-fledged social media "fast."** Set a time goal—one day, several days, or a week—and resist the urge to check social media. If you think it would be better to refrain altogether, consider deleting one or more social media accounts.

3 Control Your Response

Even with healthy filters in place, unwanted and unhelpful messages are sure to get through. You will still encounter offensive or oppressive communication from people, news, social media, and even your own thoughts. This is especially true when negative people are an unavoidable part of your life, as in Leslie's case with her mother. When you can't reduce your exposure to a negative person, speaking up may reduce the negativity they spew on you:

- Tell a gossipy coworker that you don't want to hear all the office drama anymore.
- Gently explain to a parent who keeps mentioning your weight that you need a break and will gladly talk about anything else.
- Let your spouse know that belittling comments are unwelcome and that the next time you hear them, you'll remove yourself from the conversation.

Establishing healthy boundaries will protect your heart and help to preserve your relationships. In the meantime, give yourself permission to reject negative messages and the emotions they awaken in you. In fact, responding with affirming messages to yourself, out loud, can help:

- "I reject that criticism. There's no truth in it."
- "I reject the fear I'm feeling since hearing news reports about the latest violent acts. By practicing vigilance, I can be informed without being afraid."

When negative messages are coming from your own self-talk, it's important to call them out and replace them with positive ones. After all, if you heard a friend or child speaking hurtful untruths about themselves, wouldn't you step in to correct the message? Don't love yourself any less.

4 Take Action

Not every negative message deserves to be rejected or dismissed altogether. Sometimes we don't need to reject the message itself as much as reject a misguided interpretation of the message. Does the message come as an indicator that there is something to consider and address? Do you need to apologize? Express appreciation? Talk through a conflict? Consider the following filter as an example:

- "I reject the idea that I'm somehow a bad person because [name] was displeased with me. Everyone makes mistakes, and everyone has an opinion. I'll make amends as needed, but I can do so without feeling overwhelmed."

When a message reveals something we need to address, our anxiety will be prolonged if we procrastinate or ignore the matter. Therefore, it's wise to take proper action in a timely manner.

■ ■ ■

Feeling powerless is a major contributor to burnout, but when you choose not to live at the mercy of a barrage of negative messages, you may be surprised at the result. Be creative, courageous, and bold as you filter the messages you face each day and set healthy boundaries. Taking charge of this area of your life will indeed have a positive impact on your peace of mind.

WHATEVER IS TRUE, WHATEVER IS NOBLE, WHATEVER IS RIGHT, WHATEVER IS PURE, WHATEVER IS LOVELY, WHATEVER IS ADMIRABLE—IF ANYTHING IS EXCELLENT OR PRAISEWORTHY—THINK ABOUT SUCH THINGS.

Philippians 4:8

BURNOUT BUSTERS

1. **For two days, track your social media and traditional media usage.** You might be surprised at how many hours are spent absorbing messages, images, and news. Your phone and other devices might have time-tracking functions, but if not, you can keep a written log.
2. **Next, add a "Negative Messages" column to your log.** For two days, write down sources of negative, upsetting, or worrying messages you were exposed to via technology. Then you can make the wise decision to avoid these outlets.
3. **Replace negative messages with positive affirmations and healthy boundaries.** On index cards or your phone, write a list of affirmations that counteract negative messaging you've been exposed to. Include helpful quotes from inspirational books or Scripture, if desired. Every morning, speak the affirmations aloud and determine what actions you will take to establish boundaries.

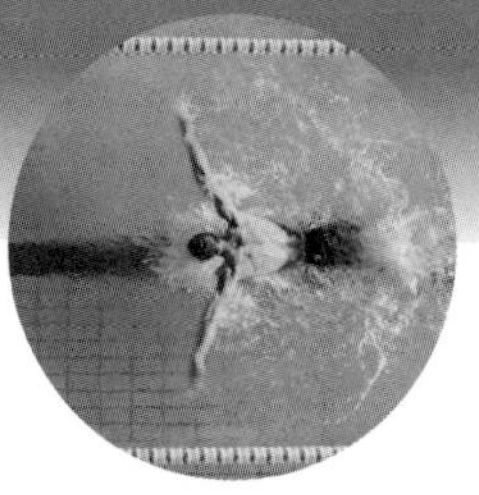

KEY 6

Choose to Replenish Yourself

Earlier I shared how I nearly lost myself for a time to burnout and depression. I told you how my family and friends intervened and helped me enforce healthy boundaries, involving many of the same methods I've already described. During that process, I learned—or rather relearned—that recovery from any significant emotional challenge happens with daily and deliberate choices.

There is nothing more exciting than realizing that the future can be what you choose to make it. Yes, unforeseen challenges will always be part of the fabric of life. But those need not have the final say in how you experience the world. That power belongs to you. Let me offer a list of eight actions you can take that will help you move out of burnout and into a new season of thriving—one decision at a time.

A Path of Refreshment

1 Have Faith in God

As the book of Hebrews assures us, "Faith is confidence in what we hope for and assurance about what we do not see" (11:1). That writer knew what it meant to hope for something you can't yet see—and he understood that active, determined faith bridges the gap while we wait and work for the thing we want. It means we can *know* we'll have what we seek, because our faith does not rest in fate or chance or any other thing on earth. Our faith is in God, who is unfailingly good.

EVERY STEP ON THE PATH TO RECOVERY REQUIRES COURAGE AND COMMITMENT ON YOUR PART.

When well-meaning people advise you to "have faith in God" during times of crisis, they often make it sound simple, as if it's possible to magically "have" something so elusive on command. That's nearly as unhelpful as telling someone who's suffering from burnout to "hang in there" or "keep going, for this too shall pass."

As we just discussed, every step on the path to recovery requires courage and commitment on your part—all summed up in one powerful word: *choice*. Before you can tap into the healing potential of the remedies you're offered, you must choose to pursue them, and faith in God is no different. It's not an ethereal "thing" we try to grasp; it's purposefully connecting with God.

Pursuing faith in God by having a relationship with him gives a jolt of energy that activates our spiritual and emotional immune systems like nothing else can. How? By opening the door to hope—something lost to almost everyone who suffers from burnout. The hope that's restored when you choose faith over despair is *real*. It's the priceless assurance that the Creator loves you beyond all reason and never takes his eyes off you—even for a second.

2 Spend Time in Prayer

Choosing faith enables you to take the next step and talk with God every day. You might be wondering, *Don't you mean "pray"?* That depends on your definition of this often misunderstood word. If you mean "to mutter a stream of routine, repetitious phrases you once heard in church," then, no, that's definitely not what I mean. Or if prayer, to you, typically consists of a dreary session of complaining and self-condemnation, that's also not what I have in mind. Instead, I want you to realize that heartfelt and honest conversation with God is yours for the having.

> DON'T WORRY ABOUT ANYTHING; INSTEAD, PRAY ABOUT EVERYTHING. TELL GOD WHAT YOU NEED, AND THANK HIM FOR ALL HE HAS DONE. THEN YOU WILL EXPERIENCE GOD'S PEACE, WHICH EXCEEDS ANYTHING WE CAN UNDERSTAND.
>
> Philippians 4:6-7 NLT

God is like a father who gleefully pulls out his wallet to show off photos of all his lovely children. And as his child, God wants to hear about how you've fought to keep going under so much pressure. What would you tell him about your small and large victories along the way? Your dreams and ambitions beyond burnout? Would you ask some tough questions? Tell him what you fear? What you love? What you want? Would you laugh and cry together? Perhaps best of all, when talking with God, you can ask for wisdom and guidance amid your struggles. Everyone on earth could use divine direction and understanding in their daily lives—and this is especially true for those battling burnout.

3 Commit to Optimism and Thankfulness

Dozens of studies show that optimists fare better than pessimists in most every area of life, including work, school, sports, and family. Positive people are likely to achieve more goals, handle stress more wisely, overcome burnout more quickly, and manage problems with far greater effectiveness.

It's interesting to note that optimism is fostered by gratitude, and gratitude helps us live with hope. That's why it's hard to imagine a more effective soul medicine than a spirit of thankfulness. Medieval Christian philosopher Meister Eckhart said, "If the only prayer you ever say in your entire life is thank you, it will be enough." The list of things we can and should be thankful for—even in our darkest moments—is practically inexhaustible. Granted, sometimes being weighed down by severe burnout makes it hard to be grateful for the big things in life, so start with the little ones. The more whimsical, the better.

For example, I am grateful for the breeze that blows in from the Puget Sound; herbal tea from the Red Twig café; and the moments my wife reaches out to hold my hand during our evening walks. How about you? Try saying thank you—out loud and with gusto—for teriyaki sauce or butterflies or kites or Mozart; for hot showers and soft towels; roller coasters, baseball, fireworks, tulips poking out of the dirt, a child's unrestrained giggle ... anything that makes you smile.

4 Reclaim Your Desires

It's remarkable how often people have trouble expressing their basic needs and desires. Somehow becoming an adult teaches us that our goals are secondary to everything and everyone else. It's true there are times when we must work hard and sacrifice short-term satisfaction, but if this becomes a habit, problems start to manifest—like burnout.

To test yourself for lost connection to your desires, take out a piece of paper and write, "I want ____________." Then make a list of all the words you might use to fill in the blank. The only rule is that each item must reflect something you want for yourself—not someone else. The desires can be practical ("I want a car that starts every time I turn the key") or more extravagant ("I want the beachside vacation I've dreamed of for years"). Don't overthink your desires—let them flow—and don't stop until you've listed at least twenty.

Now consider: Does this exercise make you uncomfortable? Do you find yourself thinking you don't deserve what's on your list? Is there a part of you that scoffs, "Yeah right, like *that's* ever going to happen"? Do you worry what others might think if you suddenly indulged yourself by pursuing something on the list? Does your memory replay all the bad things that happened the last time you dared to express your desires and act on them?

GIVE YOURSELF PERMISSION TO REACH FOR YOUR DESIRES, AND BURNOUT WILL TAKE A BACK SEAT.

If you answered yes to any of these questions, then it's likely burnout has stolen your desires from you—and it's time to take them back. Begin by looking again at the items on your list. How many are things that you once loved but stopped doing because life or naysayers got in the way? Give yourself permission to reach for your desires, and burnout will start to take a back seat. Reacquainting yourself with your wants and wishes will enable you to dream again.

5 Revive Your Purpose

Chances are that burnout has caused you to reevaluate just about every aspect of your life, including your purpose and calling. That's healthy, because burnout can teach us valuable lessons about how we want to live our lives in the future.

Now is an excellent time to pause and take a close look at what you have previously considered your purpose in life. You might find that your purpose remains the same—it just needs to be pursued with a more reasonable and healthy approach. Or it could be that you discover God and your own heart are leading you in a whole new direction.

Many people hear the word *purpose* and think it applies only to epic, world-changing work. Not so. I define purpose as the *one unique thing* we each have to offer the world, no matter how big or small. Its absence might not make headlines, but it absolutely would be missed by those who stand to benefit from our gifts.

Your personal purpose may be to pour all your energy and creativity into raising healthy children; to teach watercolor painting to residents in a retirement center; to be the most caring and conscientious insurance agent your clients have ever known; or to teach preschool in a way that fills children with self-respect and self-confidence. The possibilities are infinite. Only you can know which one best describes you.

Here's the secret to finding your purpose: Start by looking again at the list you just made of things you want in life. Chances are, what you're meant to do now is something you couldn't stop doing as a younger person but have since abandoned along the way. Or it may be something that you didn't dare put on the list, but it still tugs at your sleeve anyway. Finding and following your purpose will do wonders to lift the emotional deadweight of burnout and get you out of bed on a dreary Monday morning.

6 Rediscover the Power of Fun

It's safe to say that one thing you forgot through your struggle with burnout is how to have *fun*. At the mention of the word, it's easy to roll your eyes in exhaustion and mumble that "fun" is for other people. The best you can hope for, you think, is not to be disappointed.

I know, because that's how I felt after all my senses—including my sense of humor—were bleached and hung out to dry by burnout. It was as if the candy had been stripped out of life and only a mouthful of dry cotton was left. When you live like that for very long, words like *fun, play, pleasure,* and *enjoyment* start to sound like a foreign language.

It's instructive to notice that the word *enjoyment* refers to the process of taking pleasure in something. *Process. Taking.* These are active words, things we purposely do and participate in. You can sit and wait for joy to strike spontaneously (and it sometimes does), but why do so when you can make it happen? As with the many other healthy actions we've discussed, the power of fun is triggered by choice. I appreciate the perspective shared by science journalist Catherine Price in her book *The Power of Fun*:

> We've been conditioned to believe that the pursuit of fun—particularly *our own* fun—is frivolous, selfish, and self-indulgent, even immature and childish.... We think that if we're focused on fun, we're not paying enough attention to the world's problems or doing enough to help other people.... When you add in the time that's required to fulfill the obligations of adult life—going to work, doing your taxes, cleaning the house, raising

> kids—it's understandable that fun ends up as an afterthought....
>
> ... If we want our own lives to be satisfying and joyful, True Fun isn't optional. It shouldn't be an afterthought. It should be our guiding star.[21]

To rediscover the power of fun, start by silencing your inner critic, who pronounces judgment on every possible source of fun ... before you even try it! A rafting excursion? Too wet, too dangerous. A salsa dance class with friends? Too embarrassing. A day at the amusement park? Too childish, too expensive, too loud, too many lines. On top of all this, it seems there simply isn't time for fun when you're facing pressures and demands on so many fronts. The good news is that it's possible to replace objections like these with a determined decision to "just do it." Will this test the boundaries of your comfort zone? Of course. That's what makes it fun!

TO REDISCOVER THE POWER OF FUN, START BY SILENCING YOUR INNER CRITIC.

Throughout your week, make room for humor and lightheartedness. Turn off the news and start a romantic-comedy movie marathon, or binge on old sitcom episodes. Spend time around people who make you laugh and push you to lighten up. Make it your mission to laugh and smile so readily that people begin to wonder what you know that they don't. It's up to you: Sit on shore, or grab a surfboard and play.

7 Reset Your Pace

It's safe to say that the pace of your life over the previous months and years contributed to pulling you into burnout. It could probably be described as frantic, wearying, nonstop, draining, unrelenting—add your own adjective.

Many people rarely give themselves permission to stop and reevaluate their activity, resenting anything that hinders forward motion. But as already discussed, now is the time to take stock of your priorities and obligations. Reflect on where and how you spend your time to determine what is necessary and what is negotiable.

People act either to create something they desire or to avoid something they fear. What do your actions say about what you desire and what you fear? These are your true priorities. Now compare what you want your priorities to be with what your priorities actually are. The more out of alignment these are, the more you live at odds with yourself. And the more you live at odds with yourself, the more stress you'll have.

Resetting your pace may seem like an exercise in reducing the amount of things you do. However, finding balance in life is about making sure the things you do provide meaning and purpose. Burnout happens by doing not merely too many things but also too many of the wrong things and not enough of the right things. Looking at your life through this filter can help you determine which priorities to keep and which to let go of.

FIVE CATEGORIES OF RESTORATION

Our bodies and emotions were not meant to function in a perpetual state of stress. We cannot flourish in a depleted state. What can you do to refill your tank in each area that burnout affects—your *emotional*, *spiritual*, *physical*, *relational*, and *mental health*? As you recover from burnout, consider the following ideas gleaned from my own experience, and remember that intentional choices lead to lasting changes.

1. **Emotional Health.** I learned that my emotional tank emptied faster than any other area. This meant I needed to take intentional time alone to engage in activities that recharged my emotional life. What are some activities that will help you do this?

2. **Spiritual Health.** I learned that my spiritual tank needed daily filling with prayer, Scripture reading, and other spiritual practices. I also embraced the rhythm of work and rest that God designed us to follow. I learned to enjoy the gift of rest without feeling guilty for breaking away from work. What can you do daily and weekly to revive your spiritual tank?

3. **Physical Health.** I intentionally invested in healthy sleep patterns, a consistent exercise routine, and a diet of nutritious foods. These were essential for me to experience wellness in every other area of my life. What can you do to fill up your physical tank?

4. **Relational Health.** I needed to strengthen my family relationships, investing in communication and recreation with my wife, sons, and other family members. And I needed to lean into a few close friendships as a safe place to find support. What can you do to revitalize your relational tank?

5. **Mental Health.** Because my mental tank was normally the last area to empty, mental exhaustion became a warning sign that I was depleted. I would get together with close friends over coffee to talk about what we had been reading or journaling about. Our discussions weren't overly heavy but were enough to keep my mind activated. How about for you? What can you do to refresh your mental tank?

As I answered these questions for myself, I made a number of life-giving deliberate choices that allowed me to not only heal but also maintain wellness for the years ahead. Hopefully the examples provided here will inspire you to make your own healthy choices that will replenish these vital life categories.

8 Recruit Allies

I have often drawn a direct connection between having healthy relationships and whole-person wellness. It's a good idea to develop three close relationships based on trust, open communication, and mutual support. The irony is that burnout often causes a person to withdraw from others and put up a shield of protection against any further harm or obligation. This is a natural response, and in some cases, wise.

ONE OF THE MOST DIFFICULT CHALLENGES OF BURNOUT IS ISOLATION.

Yet one of the most difficult challenges of burnout is isolation, which can lead to unhealthy habits and thought patterns that constantly reinforce emotions of hopelessness and despair. We need a community of caring people who will provide encouragement and bolster our sense of self-worth.

Consider developing a few new relationships or strengthening your friendships with people who already love you and care about you. Invest in relationships with those who will pick you up when you're feeling down and celebrate life's victories with you.

BURNOUT BUSTERS

1. **Ask for divine help.** As Jesus told his followers, "Everyone who asks receives; the one who seeks finds; and to the one who knocks, the door will be opened" (Matthew 7:8). There is no more powerful prayer than a simple plea for help. Also ask for God's wisdom as you seek to overcome burnout and make decisions that will foster healing.

2. **Regularly pause to say thank you.** Gratitude is a key component in healing from burnout. Yet many people overlook the blessings in their life or can't embrace the good when they feel so bad. Make a choice each day to be grateful. Before you go to sleep, review the gifts that came your way. On a walk with a friend, mention some things you're thankful for. Keep a gratitude journal and pray with a particular focus on thankfulness.

3. **Celebrate your successes.** As you experience successes in your efforts to overcome burnout, stop and savor the moments. Celebrate by going out to dinner with friends. Treat yourself to fun or pampering activities. Journal about the milestones in your journey—discovering a healthier way of seeing things, letting go of a grudge, improving your diet, beginning a workout program, getting to bed earlier, tackling problems sooner rather than later.

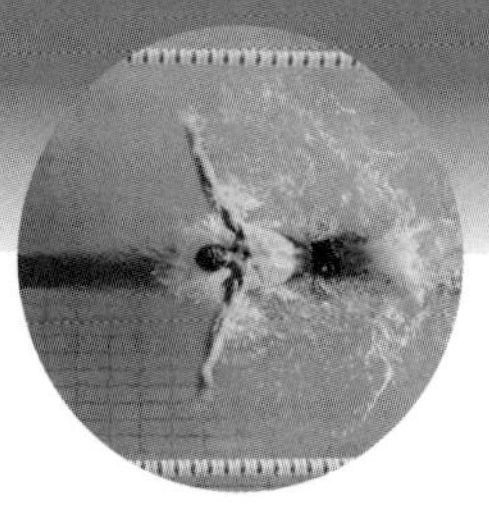

A CLOSING WORD

The Master of Balance

I grew up in a family that attended church and read Scripture together. I heard all the Bible stories about Jesus leading his disciples, teaching and healing crowds of people, and managing uptight religious leaders who were hostile to his message. Working as a mental health professional over the years, I have never failed to be inspired and impressed at how skillfully Jesus managed the many demands in his life, always remaining unhurried and balanced.

Jesus had a schedule filled with things to do and places to go. He frequently met new people in his travels, each with their own problems and requests. He was also a polarizing figure—many of the religious leaders hated him because so many regular folks loved him. Although the term *burnout* wouldn't be coined until centuries after Jesus's time on earth, his lifestyle and calling put him at risk for physical exhaustion, emotional depletion, and relational challenges. At the same time, Jesus understood his humanity and limitations. He knew that with the demands of teaching, leading, serving, and healing, he needed rhythms of rest and refueling. It's interesting to note that the Bible records Jesus's methods for withstanding the stress:

- "He withdrew by boat privately to a solitary place." (Matthew 14:13)
- "Very early in the morning, while it was still dark, Jesus got up, left the house and went off to a solitary place, where he prayed." (Mark 1:35)
- "Because so many people were coming and going that they did not even have a chance to eat, he said to them, 'Come with me by yourselves to a quiet place and get some rest.'" (Mark 6:31)
- "Jesus made his disciples get into the boat and go on ahead of him to Bethsaida, while he dismissed the crowd. After leaving them, he went up on a mountainside to pray." (Mark 6:45–46)
- "Jesus often withdrew to lonely places and prayed." (Luke 5:16)

A theme emerges in these descriptions: Jesus withdrew to solitary places to be quiet. To rest. To pray. To get away from demands for a while. Jesus navigated the pressures of his calling in a healthy way: He rested physically, and he replenished his soul in quietness. He nurtured his spiritual life and relationship with God. Jesus exemplified this life-changing principle for all of us: *We need to break away so we don't break down.*

WE WERE NOT CREATED TO WORK AND STRIVE ENDLESSLY.

Jesus mirrored the pattern of creation—work, rest, thrive. We can learn from this healthy pattern to prevent burnout or recover from it. We can acknowledge our limitations, recognizing that we are human—not superhuman. We were not created to work and strive endlessly. We were not created to do everything for everyone. We were not created to try to meet unrealistic expectations.

One of our society's most irrational ideas is that we should always push the limits: *Maximize your busyness, speed, and efficiency—then increase it another 10 percent!* While this approach makes us feel productive, it is damaging to every area of our lives. We were created to work and rest, sow and reap.

Allowing for *margin* in life means having a buffer against the things that deplete you. It means resolving to create valuable rhythms of rest and replenishment for your soul. Breaking away to create margin might include:

- **A daily rest.** This is an intentional commitment to set aside "reset" breaks in the day and cultivate healthy sleep patterns at night. You may protest, "I hardly have time to do the laundry—when am I going to rest?" But if you are not proactive and deliberate about taking time to rest, the consequences will catch up with you.
- **A weekly Sabbath.** This is an intentional day to rest and replenish your soul. God established a wonderful pattern at the time of creation—take a day off to rest and enjoy all that is good. "God had finished his work of creation, so he rested from all his work" (Genesis 2:2 NLT). Give yourself permission to do the same!
- **A yearly vacation.** This is an intentional time away, once or multiple times per year, to disconnect from work, enjoy your loved ones, and savor life for several continuous days.

Hopefully you noticed the recurring word in this list: *intentional*. In our hectic and harried world, these replenishment breaks don't magically materialize. It's up to each of us to carefully and courageously make them happen. As we do, we will reawaken to the abundant life that Jesus invited us into and promised to fulfill:

I have come that they may have life,
and have it to the full.

John 10:10

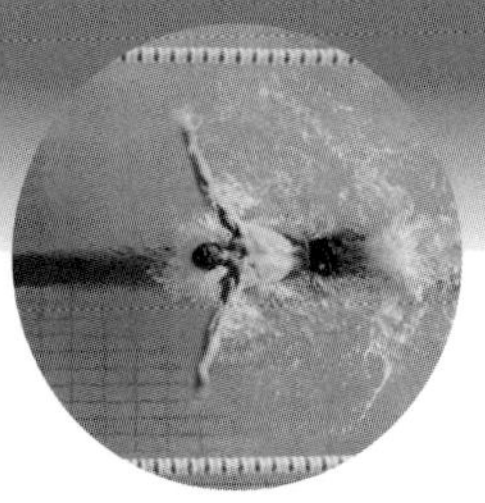

Notes

1 See Rajvinder Samra, "Brief History of Burnout," *BMJ* (December 27, 2018), *https://doi.org/10.1136/bmj.k5268,* and Flávio Fernandes Fontes, "Herbert J. Freudenberger and the Making of Burnout as a Psychopathological Syndrome," *Memorandum Memória e História em Psicologia* 37 (December 2020): 3–5, *https://www.researchgate.net/publication/346586006_Herbert_J_Freudenberger_and_the_making_of_burnout_as_a_psychopathological_syndrome.*

2 "Burnout," *Psychology Today: https://www.psychologytoday.com/us/basics/burnout.*

3 Tracy Brower, "Burnout Is a Worldwide Problem: 5 Ways Work Must Change," July 24, 2022, *Forbes: https://www.forbes.com/sites/tracybrower/2022/07/24/burnout-is-a-worldwide-problem-5-ways-work-must-change/?sh=7e5b2b906c1e.*

4 Steve Hatfield et al., "The C-Suite's Role in Well-Being," June 22, 2022, *Deloitte Insights: https://www2.deloitte.com*

/us/en/insights/topics/leadership/employee-wellness-in-the -corporate-workplace.html.

5 "38% of U.S. Pastors Have Thought about Quitting Full-Time Ministry in the Past Year," November 16, 2021, *Barna: https://www.barna.com/research/pastors-well -being/.*

6 "Stress in America 2023," *American Psychological Association: http://www.apa.org/news/press/releases /stress/2015/snapshot.aspx.*

7 Bernard Marr, "Why Too Much Data Is Stressing Us Out," November 25, 2015, *Forbes: https://www.forbes.com/sites /bernardmarr/2015/11/25/why-too-much-data-is-stressing -us-out/#5325947f7630.*

8 "Stress in America 2022," *American Psychological Association: https://www.apa.org/news/press/releases /stress/2022/concerned-future-inflation#:~:text=Around %20a%20third%20of%20adults,to%20report%20feeling%20 this%20way.*

9 George M. Slavich and Michael R. Irwin, "From Stress to Inflammation and Major Depressive Disorder: A Social Signal Transduction Theory of Depression," *Psychological Bulletin* 140, no. 3 (2014): 774–815, *https://www.ncbi.nlm .nih.gov/pmc/articles/PMC4006295/.*

10 Hara Estroff Marano, "Why We Procrastinate," July 1, 2005, *Psychology Today: https://www.psychologytoday.com /us/articles/200507/why-we-procrastinate.*

11 Julia Cameron, *The Artist's Way* (New York: Jeremy P. Tarcher/Putnam, 2002), 120.

12 Neel Burton, "Building Confidence and Self-Esteem," April 28, 2020, *Psychology Today: https://www.psychologytoday.com/us/blog/hide-and-seek/201205/building-confidence-and-self-esteem.*

13 Charles M. Schulz, *Peanuts*, March 19, 2010.

14 Marie Kondo, *The Life-Changing Magic of Tidying Up* (Berkeley, CA: Ten Speed Press, 2014), 42.

15 A. M. Coniaris, "The Four Friends," *Message of the Sunday Gospels*, vol. 2 (Minneapolis: Light & Life Publishing, 1983), 8.

16 Megan Clapp et al., "Gut Microbiota's Effect on Mental Health: The Gut-Brain Axis," *Clinics and Practice* 7, no. 4 (September 15, 2017): 987, *https://doi.org/10.4081/cp.2017.987.*

17 "Exercise for Stress and Anxiety," *Anxiety & Depression Association of America: https://www.health.harvard.edu/blog/can-exercise-help-treat-anxiety-2019102418096.*

18 See U.S. Department of Health and Human Services, *Physical Activity Guidelines for Americans*, 2nd ed. (2018), 8, *Health.gov: https://health.gov/sites/default/files/2019-09/Physical_Activity_Guidelines_2nd_edition.pdf.*

19 Sandee LaMotte, "Sleep Deprivation Affects Nearly Half of American Adults, Study Finds," November 8, 2022, *CNN Health: https://www.cnn.com/2022/11/08/health/sleep-deprivation-wellness/index.html.*

20 Josh Howarth, "17 Cyberbullying Facts & Statistics (2024)," November 22, 2023, *Exploding Topics: https://*

explodingtopics.com/blog/cyberbullying-stats#general-cyberbullying-stats.

21 Catherine Price, *The Power of Fun* (New York: The Dial Press, 2021), 17.

Image Credits

Images used under license from Shutterstock.com: cover, pp. 3, 5, 19, 31, 41, 53, 71, 83, 101, 107 Gorodenkoff; p. 6 Prostock-studio; p. 11 Natalia Deriabina; p. 12 Stokkete; p. 14 Katrina Lee (brain), Yana Lesnik (muscle), Alex Ghidan (human pictogram), Palsur (apple), Miki yal (palette); p. 15 Hamara; p. 16 KieferPix; p. 21 Motortion Films; pp. 22, 95 ntkris; p. 25 Mutita Narkmuang; p. 27 Monkey Business Images; p. 28 GRJ Photo; p. 33 VSM Fotografia; p. 34 Ivanko80; p. 36 Marjan Apostolovic; p. 43 Ground Picture; p. 46 frank_kie; p. 47 Samuel Borges Photography; p. 49 Konontsev Artem; p. 51 rdonar; p. 59 monticello; p. 60 Sergii Sobolevskyi; p. 63 GP PIXSTOCK; p. 68 Pixel-Shot; p. 74 zimmytws; p. 84 hxdbzxy; p. 89 gornjak; p. 90 ESB Professional; p. 93 Roman Samborskyi; p. 98 didesign021; p. 103 wavebreakmedia.

MORE RESOURCES FROM DR. GREGORY L. JANTZ

Unmasking Emotional Abuse

Six Steps to Reduce Stress

Ten Tips for Parenting the Smartphone Generation

Five Keys to Dealing with Depression

Seven Answers for Anxiety

Five Keys to Raising Boys

Freedom from Shame

Five Keys to Health and Healing

When a Loved One Is Addicted

40 Answers for Teens' Top Questions

Social Media and Depression

Rebuilding Trust after Betrayal

How to Deal with Toxic People

The Power of Connection

Why Failure Is Never Final

Find Your Purpose in Life

Here Today, Ghosted Tomorrow

Beyond Burnout

www.hendricksonrose.com